interchange

THIRD EDITION

Jack C. Richards

Intro B

WORKBOOK

CAMBRIDGE UNIVERSITY PRESS
Cambridge, New York, Melbourne, Madrid, Cape Town,
Singapore, São Paulo, Delhi, Mexico City

Cambridge University Press
32 Avenue of the Americas, New York, NY 10013–2473, USA

www.cambridge.org
Information on this title: www.cambridge.org/9780521601573

First published 2005
18th printing 2013

Interchange Third Edition Intro Workbook B has been developed from *New Interchange*
Intro Workbook B, first published by Cambridge University Press in 2000.

Printed in Hong Kong, China, by Golden Cup Printing Company Limited

A catalog record for this publication is available from the British Library.

ISBN..978-0-521-60157-3 workbook

Art direction, book design, photo research, and layout services: Adventure House, NYC

Contents

Acknowledgments

Illustrations

Keith Bendis 58, 81
Adam Hurwitz 49, 51, 52, 55, 66, 93
Randy Jones 57, 68, 71, 74, 77, 82, 94, 96

Ben Shannon 64
Dan Vasconcellos 63, 67, 69, 76, 79, 84, 92

Photo credits

50 (*left to right*) © Microzoa/Getty Images; © Brian Hagiwara/Getty Images
53 (*top to bottom*) © Akira Sakimoto/Alamy; © Richard Gross/The Stock Market
54 (*left to right*) © Roy Morsch/Corbis; © Steven Needham/Envision; © Arthur Beck/The Stock Market
56 (*top to bottom*) © Robert Brenner/Photo Edit; © Donald Dietz/Stock Boston
59 (*clockwise from top right*) © Richard Hutchings/Photo Edit; © Getty Images; © David Turnley/Corbis
60 © Nancy Ney/Corbis
61 (*left to right*) © Superstock; © Vito Palmisano/Getty Images; © Jerry Howard/Stock Boston; © Henryk Kaiser/Envision
65 (*left to right, top to bottom*) © Corbis; © Michael Mahovlich/Masterfile; © Alamy; © Alamy; © Martin Riedel/Getty Images; © Dick Luria/Getty Images; © Adamsmith/Getty Images; © David Young-Wolff/Photo Edit; © Michael Mahovlich/Masterfile

70 (*top to bottom*) © Steven Ogilvy; © LWA-Stephen Welstead/Corbis
73 © Richard B. Levine/Newscom
80 © SW Production/Index Stock
83 © George Shelley/Corbis
85 © Alfredo Maiquez/Lonely Planet
86 (*top to bottom*) © Corbis; © Roger Ressmeyer/Corbis; © Gavin Hellier/Alamy
87 (*left to right, top to bottom*) © PhotoFest; © PhotoFest/Icon Archives; © PhotoFest; © Bettmann/Corbis; © PhotoFest; © PhotoFest
89 © Alamy
90 © Bob Daemmrich/Stock Boston
91 (*left to right*) © Masterfile; © Pierre Arsenault/Masterfile
94 © Punchstock
95 © Stock Boston

9 Broccoli is good for you.

1 *Write the names of the foods.*

Fruit

1. _____mangoes_____
2. _____
3. _____
4. _____

Vegetables

5. _____
6. _____
7. _____
8. _____

Grains

9. _____
10. _____
11. _____

Fat, oil, and sugar

12. _____
13. _____
14. _____

Dairy

15. _____
16. _____

Meat and other protein

17. _____
18. _____
19. _____
20. _____

2 *What foods do you like? What foods don't you like? Write sentences.*

1. fruit   *I like apples and mangoes. I don't like bananas.*

2. vegetables   _____

3. meat and other protein   _____

4. dairy   _____

5. grains   _____

6. drinks   _____

7. desserts   _____

3 *Are these foods good for you or bad for you? Write sentences.*

1. strawberries   *Strawberries are good for you.*

2. cake   _____

3. lettuce   _____

4. fish   _____

5. potato chips   _____

6. eggs   _____

7. potatoes   _____

8. pizza   _____

9. beans   _____

10. yogurt   _____

11. cookies   _____

12. broccoli   _____

4 **Complete the conversations with some or any.**

1. A: What do you want for dinner?

    B: Let's make __some__ pasta with
    tomato sauce.

    A: Good idea. Do we have _____ meat?

    B: Well, we have _____ beef, but
    I don't want _____ meat in the sauce.
    Let's get _____ tomatoes and onions.

    A: OK. Do we need _____ green peppers
    for the sauce?

    B: Yes, let's get _____ peppers.
    Oh, and _____ garlic, too.

    A: Great. We have _____ spaghetti,
    so we don't need _____ pasta.

    B: Yeah, but let's get _____ bread.
    And _____ cheese, too.

2. A: What do you eat for breakfast?

    B: Well, first, I have fruit – _____ grapes
    or strawberries.

    A: That sounds good. Do you have _____
    eggs or bacon?

    B: No, I don't eat _____ eggs or meat
    in the morning.

    A: Really? Do you have anything else?

    B: Well, I usually have _____ bread,
    but I don't use _____ butter.

    A: Do you drink anything in the morning?

    B: I always have _____ juice and coffee.
    I don't put _____ sugar in my coffee,
    but I like _____ milk in it.

5 **What do you need to make these foods? What don't you need? Write sentences.**

1. a chicken sandwich
   You need some bread, chicken, lettuce, and
   mayonnaise. You don't need any cheese.

2. a cheeseburger
   _____
   _____

3. chicken soup
   _____
   _____

4. a vegetable salad
   _____
   _____

5. a fruit salad
   _____
   _____

6. your favorite food
   _____
   _____

6 *Food habits*

A Put the adverbs in the correct places.

1. Americans put cream in their coffee. (often)
   Americans often put cream in their coffee.

2. Some people in Korea eat pickled vegetables for
   breakfast. (always)
   _____

3. In China, people put sugar in their tea. (seldom)
   _____

4. In England, people put milk in their tea. (usually)
   _____

5. In Japan, people have fish for breakfast. (sometimes)
   _____

6. Brazilians make drinks with fruit. (often)
   _____

7. In Canada, people have salad for breakfast. (hardly ever)
   _____

8. Some Mexicans eat pasta. (never)
   _____

B Rewrite the sentences in part A. Use your own information.

1. Americans often put cream in their coffee.
   I hardly ever put cream in my coffee. /
   I sometimes put milk in my coffee.

2. _____
3. _____
4. _____
5. _____
6. _____
7. _____
8. _____

7 Do you often have these things for dinner? Write sentences. Use the adverbs in the box.

never   hardly ever   sometimes   often   usually   always

1. cheese   *I hardly ever have cheese for dinner.*
2. milk
3. coffee
4. eggs
5. yogurt
6. rice
7. beans
8. chicken

8 Answer the questions with your own information.

1. What's your favorite kind of food?

2. What's your favorite restaurant?

3. What do you usually have at your favorite restaurant?

4. Do you ever make dinner for your family?

5. What's your favorite snack?

Chinese food   Mexican food   Italian food

I can't ice-skate very well.

1 Sports

A Complete the crossword puzzle. Write the names of the sports.

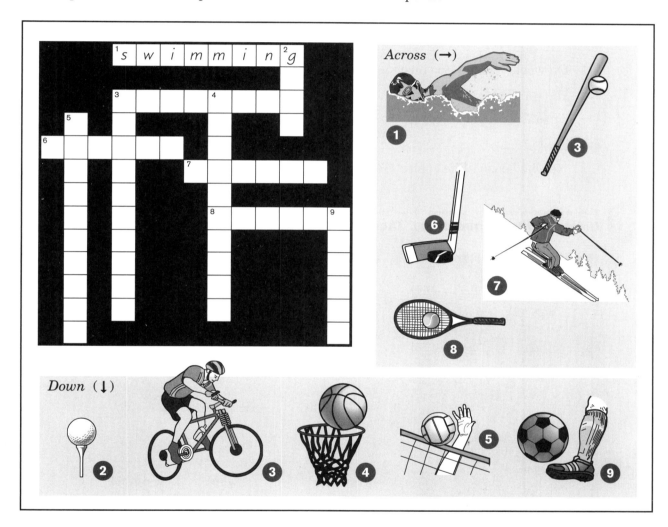

Across (→)

Down (↓)

B Which sports in part A follow *go*? Which sports follow *play*? Complete the chart.

go	play	
swimming		

2 Complete the conversation. Use the questions in the box.

> ☐ Who do you practice with? ☐ Does your sister play volleyball, too?
> ☑ Do you like sports? ☐ When do you usually practice?
> ☐ What sports do you like?

Joe: *Do you like sports?*

Liz: Yes, I do. I like them a lot.

Joe: Really? _____

Liz: Well, I love volleyball.

Joe: _____

Liz: On weekends. I'm too busy on weekdays.

Joe: _____

Liz: I usually practice with my friends from school.

Joe: _____

Liz: No, she doesn't like sports. She thinks they're boring.

3 Unscramble the questions. Then answer with your own information.

1. you   do   like   baseball
   Do you like baseball?
   _____

2. sports   what   do   watch   you
   _____
   _____

3. you   play   sports   what   do
   _____
   _____

4. swimming   do   you   how often   go
   _____
   _____

5. do   with   who   sports   you   play
   _____
   _____

4 Write questions and answers about these people.

Andrew

1. *Can Andrew fix a car?*
   No, he can't.

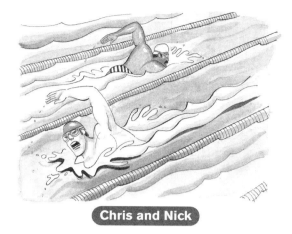
Chris and Nick

2. _____

Rebecca

3. _____
   _____

Jennifer

4. _____
   _____

Sue and Lisa

5. _____
   _____

Alan

6. _____
   _____

5 **Write sentences about these people. Use** can, can't, **and** but.

1. *She can play the guitar, but*
   she can't play the piano.

2. _____
   _____

3. _____
   _____

4. _____
   _____

6 **Choose the correct responses.**

1. A: Do you like the guitar?

   B: *No, I don't.* _____

   - Yes, I can.
   - No, I don't.

2. A: Who do you play tennis with?

   B: _____

   - I do.
   - My sister.

3. A: Who can sing?

   B: _____

   - I can.
   - Yes, I can.

4. A: Where do you go skiing?

   B: _____

   - In winter.
   - In Colorado.

Can *or* can't?

A Can you do these things? Check (✓) *can* or *can't*.

	can	can't
1. cook	☐	☐
2. dance	☐	☐
3. draw	☐	☐
4. drive a car	☐	☐
5. play the piano	☐	☐
6. play tennis	☐	☐
7. speak two languages	☐	☐
8. swim	☐	☐
9. tell good jokes	☐	☐
10. use a computer	☐	☐

B Write sentences about the things in part A.

1. *I can't cook at all.*
2. *I can dance really well.*
3. _____
4. _____
5. _____
6. _____
7. _____
8. _____
9. _____
10. _____

8 *Write each sentence a different way. Use the sentences in the box.*

> ☑ I hardly ever ski.   ☐ I love it.   ☐ He can play sports well.
> ☐ I need a bike.   ☐ He can't sing at all. ☐ He has many talents.

1. I don't ski very often.
   I hardly ever ski.

2. He has a lot of abilities.
   _____

3. I really like it.
   _____

4. He's a terrible singer.
   _____

5. I don't have a bike.
   _____

6. He's a great athlete.
   _____

9 *Answer these questions with short answers. Use your own information.*

1. Can you speak English well?   _____
2. Can you speak Spanish?   _____
3. Can you ride a bike?   _____
4. Do you like music?   _____
5. Are you a good student?   _____
6. Do you like your English class?   _____
7. Can you sing any Japanese songs?   _____
8. Do you ever go skiing?   _____
9. Do you ever go swimming?   _____
10. Can you design a Web page?   _____

10 *What can your classmates do? What can't they do? Write sentences.*

1. _____
2. _____
3. _____
4. _____

11 What are you going to do?

1 *Months and dates*

A Put the months in the box in time order.

☐ April ☐ December ☑ January ☐ July ☐ May ☐ October
☐ August ☐ February ☐ June ☐ March ☐ November ☐ September

1. *January*
2. _____
3. _____
4. _____

5. _____
6. _____
7. _____
8. _____

9. _____
10. _____
11. _____
12. _____

B When are the seasons in your country? Write the months for each season.

Spring	Summer	Fall	Winter

C Write each date a different way.

1. March 12th   *March twelfth*
2. April 11th   _____
3. January 16th _____
4. February 9th _____

5. October 1st   _____
6. May 22nd   _____
7. July 3rd   _____
8. August 30th   _____

2 It's January first. How old are these people going to be on their next birthdays? Write sentences.

	Alex	Anita	Peggy and Patty	You
Age now	76	25	18	_____
Birthday	March 15th	July 27th	September 6th	_____

1. *Alex is going to be seventy-seven on March fifteenth.* _____

2. _____

3. _____

4. _____

3 Read Beth's calendar. Write sentences about her plans. Use the words in parentheses.

JUNE

Sun.	Mon.	Tues.	Wed.	Thurs.	Fri.	Sat.
1	**2** play golf after work	**3** have lunch with Tony	**4**	**5**	**6**	**7** go shopping with Julie
8 meet John for dinner	**9**	**10**	**11** work late	**12**	**13** go to Sam's party	**14**
15	**16** see a movie with Tony	**17**	**18**	**19**	**20**	**21** have a family picnic
22/29	**23/30**	**24** buy Paula's birthday present	**25** go to Paula's birthday dinner	**26**	**27**	**28**

1. *On June second, she's going to play golf after work.* _____ (June 2nd)

2. _____ (June 3rd)

3. _____ (June 7th)

4. _____ (June 8th)

5. _____ (June 11th)

6. _____ (June 13th)

7. _____ (June 16th)

8. _____ (June 21st)

9. _____ (June 24th)

10. _____ (June 25th)

4 Complete these sentences. Use the correct form of **be going to** and the verbs in parentheses.

1. This _is going to be_ (be) a very busy weekend.

2. On Friday, my friend Ben and I _____ (see) a movie. After the movie, we _____ (eat) dinner at our favorite Thai restaurant.

3. On Saturday morning, my parents _____ (visit). They _____ (drive) into the city, and we _____ (go) to the art museum. I think my mother _____ (love) it, but my father _____ (not like) it. Later, we _____ (watch) a football game on television. My parents _____ (go) home after dinner.

4. On Sunday, I _____ (sleep) late. Then I _____ (read) the newspaper. On Sunday afternoon, I _____ (take) a walk. In the evening, my friend Jill and I _____ (study) together.

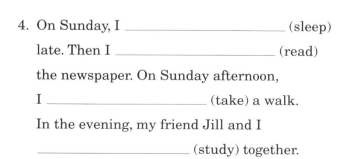

5 **Complete these conversations. Write questions with** be going to.

1. Sarah: *What are you going to do this*
   weekend?

   Eric: This weekend? I'm going to go to the
   country with my brother.

   Sarah: That's nice. _____

   _____

   Eric: We're going to stay at our friend
   Marjorie's house. She lives there.

   Sarah: Really? _____

   _____

   Eric: I think we're going to go mountain
   climbing.

   Sarah: _____

   _____

   Eric: No, Marjorie isn't going to go with
   us. She's going to go bike riding.

2. Scott: I'm going to have a birthday party for
   Tara next Saturday. Can you come?

   Emily: Sure. _____

   _____

   Scott: It's going to be at my house. Do you
   have the address?

   Emily: Yes, I do. And _____

   _____

   Scott: It's going to start at seven o'clock.

   Emily: _____

   _____

   Scott: No, Bob isn't going to be there. He
   can't come.

   Emily: That's too bad. _____

   _____

   Scott: No, I'm not going to bake a cake.
   I can't bake! I'm going to buy one.

   Emily: OK. Sounds good. See you on Saturday.

6 Next weekend

A What are these people going to do next weekend? Write sentences.

1. _They're going to go to the gym._

2. _____

3. _____

4. _____

5. _____

6. _____

7. _____

8. _____

9. _____

B What are you going to do next weekend? How about your family and friends? Write sentences.

1. _____
2. _____
3. _____
4. _____

7 *Are you going to do anything special on these holidays or special occasions? Write sentences. Use the phrases in the box or your own information.*

dance	go to a party	see my family
eat special food	go to a restaurant	sing songs
give greeting cards	have a party	stay home
give presents	have a picnic	stay up all night
go out with friends	open presents	take pictures

New Year's Eve

New Year's Day

I'm not going to go to a party. I'm going to go to a restaurant with my friends, but we're not going to stay out late.

Your next birthday

Your best friend's birthday

Valentine's Day

Your favorite holiday

12 What's the matter?

1 **Label the parts of the body. Use the words in the box.**

☐ arm	☐ leg
☐ ear	☐ mouth
☐ elbow	☐ neck
☐ eye	☐ nose
☐ fingers	☐ shoulder
☐ foot	☐ stomach
☐ hand	☐ teeth
☑ head	☐ toes

1. _____head_____

2. _____

3. _____

4. _____

5. _____

6. _____

7. _____

8. _____

9. _____

10. _____

11. _____

12. _____

13. _____

14. _____

15. _____

16. _____

2 *What's wrong with these people? Write sentences.*

1. *He has an earache.*

2. _____

3. _____

4. _____

5. _____

6. _____

3 **Complete the conversations. Use the questions and sentences in the box.**

☐ That's too bad. Are you going to see a doctor?
☐ I'm glad to hear that.
☐ How do you feel tonight?
☑ I'm fine, thanks. How about you?

☐ So, are you going to go to school tomorrow?
☐ What's wrong?
☐ Great. See you tomorrow.
☐ I hope you feel better soon.

In the afternoon

1. Jason: Hi, Lisa. How are you?

   Lisa: *I'm fine, thanks. How about you?*

   Jason: Not so good. Actually, I feel really awful.

   Lisa: _____

   Jason: I think I have the flu.

   Lisa: _____

   Jason: No, I'm going to go home and rest.

   Lisa: _____

   Jason: Thanks.

In the evening

2. Lisa: _____

   Jason: I feel much better.

   Lisa: _____

   Jason: Thanks.

   Lisa: _____

   Jason: Yes, I am.

   Lisa: _____

4 Complete the sentences with the correct medications.

1. Her eyes are very tired. She needs some _____eye drops_____ .

2. Your cough sounds terrible. Take some _____ or some _____ .

3. I have a headache, so I'm going to buy some _____ .

4. My arm is sore. I'm going to put some _____ on my arm.

5. Kristina has a stomachache, so I'm going to give her some _____ .

6. Suzie has a terrible cold. She's going to take some _____ .

5 Write each sentence a different way. Use the sentences in the box.

- ☐ My head feels terrible.
- ☐ I miss my family.
- ☑ What's wrong?
- ☐ I'm glad to hear that.
- ☐ I'm not happy.
- ☐ I'm sorry to hear that.
- ☐ I'm very tired.
- ☐ I have a sore throat.

1. What's the matter?
   What's wrong?

2. I feel sad.
   _____

3. That's too bad.
   _____

4. I'm homesick.
   _____

5. My throat is sore.
   _____

6. I have a headache.
   _____

7. That's good.
   _____

8. I'm exhausted.
   _____

6 **Give these people advice. Use the phrases in the box.**

☐ drink some water	☐ go to the grocery store	☐ have a hot drink	☐ stay up late
☐ go home early	☐ lift heavy things	☐ go outside	☑ work too hard

1. _Don't work too hard._

2. _____

3. _____

4. _____

5. _____

6. _____

7. _____

8. _____

7 Write two pieces of advice for each problem.

1. I have a cold.   _Don't go to school today. Take a cold pill._
2. I have a toothache.   _____
3. I have a sore throat.   _____
4. I have an earache.   _____
5. I have a stomachache.   _____
6. I have a backache.   _____
7. I have sore eyes.   _____
8. I'm homesick.   _____

8 Health survey

A How healthy and happy are you? Complete the survey.

How often do you . . . ?	Often	Sometimes	Hardly ever	Never
get a headache	☐	☐	☐	☐
get an earache	☐	☐	☐	☐
get a stomachache	☐	☐	☐	☐
get a cold	☐	☐	☐	☐
get the flu	☐	☐	☐	☐
stay up late	☐	☐	☐	☐
feel homesick	☐	☐	☐	☐
feel sad	☐	☐	☐	☐

B Write four sentences about your health. Use the information from the survey in part A.

Example:
1. _I hardly ever get a headache, an earache, or a stomachache._
2. _Sometimes I get a cold or the flu in the winter._
3. _I often stay up late on weekends, but I never stay up late on weekdays._
4. _Sometimes I feel a little homesick, but I hardly ever feel really sad._

1. _____
2. _____
3. _____
4. _____

13 You can't miss it.

1 *Places*

A Complete these sentences with the correct places.
Write one letter on each line.

1. We need gasoline for the car. Is there a
   _g_ _a_ _s_ _s_ _t_ _a_ _t_ _i_ _o_ _n_ near here?

2. I'm going to go to the ___ ___ ___ ___ . I need some traveler's checks.

3. I work at a ___ ___ ___ ___ ___ ___ ___ ___ . I love books, so it's a great job.

4. Are you going to the ___ ___ ___ ___ ___ ___ ___ ___ ___ ___ ? I need some stamps.

5. We don't have anything for dinner. Let's buy some food at the

   ___ ___ ___ ___ ___ ___ ___ ___ ___ ___ ___ .

6. Tomorrow we're going to go to Paris for five days. We're going to stay

   at an expensive ___ ___ ___ ___ ___ .

7. I have a stomachache. Can you buy some antacid at the ___ ___ ___ ___ ___ ___ ___ ___ ___ ?

8. Let's go out for lunch. There's a great Mexican ___ ___ ___ ___ ___ ___ ___ ___ ___ ___ downtown.

B Find and circle the places in part A in the puzzle.

```
P  H  K  T  Y  W  X  D  C  H  B  S  S  R
D  O  A  W  O  J  R  P  T  O  O  Y  R  E
F  M  S  J  D  R  U  G  S  T  O  R  E  S
S  C  K  T  F  U  Z  V  N  E  K  T  M  T
N  P  W  O  O  H  Y  P  R  L  S  E  L  A
S  K  P  U  K  F  N  S  A  Q  T  N  X  U
K  N  I  B  Y  S  F  U  Y  W  O  M  I  R
G  A  S  S  T  A  T  I  O  N  R  V  G  A
E  B  L  F  W  G  P  C  C  M  E  A  O  N
S  U  P  E  R  M  A  R  K  E  T  K  G  T
```

2 *Look at the map. Complete the sentences with the prepositions in the box.*

☐ across from   ☐ between   ☑ on
☐ behind   ☐ next to   ☐ on the corner of

1. The English school is ___on___ Catherine Street.
2. The hospital is _____ the hotel.
3. The Mexican restaurant is _____ Beatrice Street and Fourth Avenue.
4. The bank is on Barbara Street, _____ Sixth and Seventh Avenues.
5. The bookstore is _____ the English school.
6. The coffee shop is _____ the park.

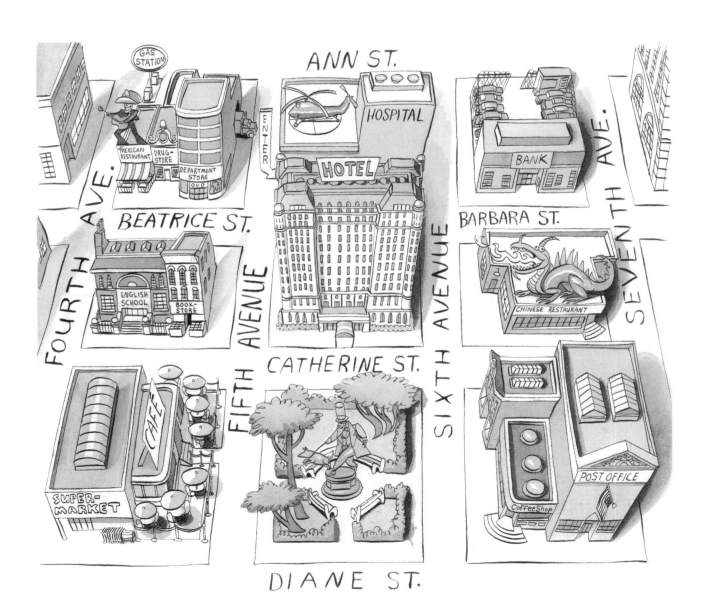

③ Where is it?

A Look at the map in Exercise 2 again. Where is each place? Write two sentences.

1. bookstore   *The bookstore is on the corner of Catherine Street and Fifth Avenue. It's next to the English school.*

2. supermarket

3. department store

4. gas station

5. Chinese restaurant

6. hotel

7. post office

8. drugstore

B Where is your school? Draw a map. Then write two sentences.

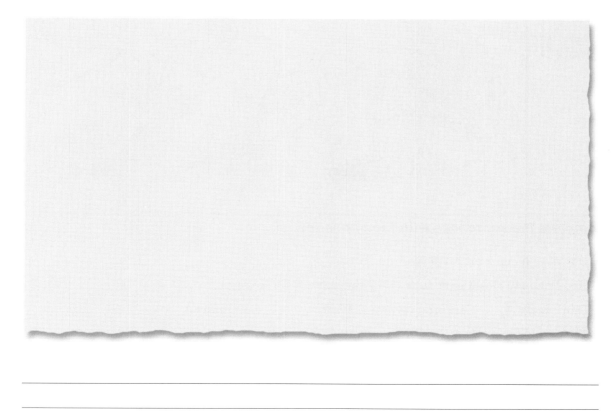

4 **Complete the conversation. Use the sentences and questions in the box.**

☐ Next to the coffee shop?   ☑ Excuse me. Can you help me?
☐ Is there a post office around here?   ☐ Where on Diane Street?
☐ Thanks a lot.

Rachel: *Excuse me. Can you help me?*

Man: Sure.

Rachel: _____

Man: Yes, there is. It's on Diane Street.

Rachel: _____

Man: It's on the corner of Diane Street and Seventh Avenue.

Rachel: _____

Man: Yes, that's right. It's right next to the coffee shop.

Rachel: _____

Man: You're welcome.

5 **Complete the sentences with the opposites.**

1. Don't turn *right* on Fifth Avenue. Turn ___left___ .

2. The Waverly Hotel isn't *in front of* the concert hall. It's _____ it.

3. Don't walk *down* Columbus Avenue. Walk _____ Columbus Avenue.

4. The museum isn't on the *left*. It's on the _____ .

5. The Empire State Building is *far* from here, but Central Park is very _____ .
   You can walk there.

6 **Look at the map. Give these people directions. Use the phrases and sentences in the box.**

Walk up/Go up . . . Street/Avenue. Turn left on . . . Street/Avenue. Walk to . . . Street/Avenue.	Walk down/Go down . . . Street/Avenue. Turn right on . . . Street/Avenue. It's on the left/right.

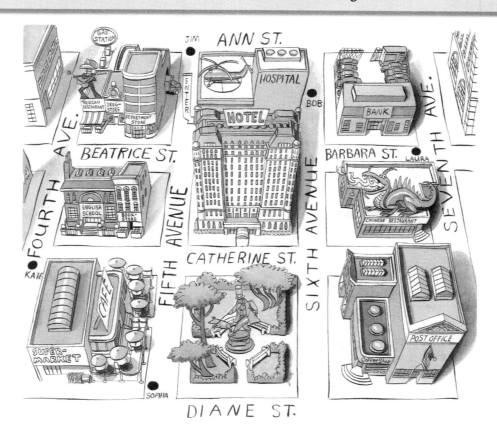

1. Sophia is looking for the Mexican restaurant.

   Go up Fifth Avenue. Turn left on Beatrice Street.

   Walk to Fourth Avenue. It's on the right.

2. Kate is looking for the post office.

   _____

   _____

3. Bob is looking for the hotel.

   _____

   _____

4. Laura is looking for the supermarket.

   _____

   _____

5. Jim is looking for the bank.

   _____

   _____

7 *Imagine you're going to have a party. Complete the invitation. Then draw a map and write directions to the party from your school.*

PARTY!

Date: _____

Time: _____

Place: _____

MAP TO THE PARTY

DIRECTIONS TO THE PARTY

Start at the school. Then ....

....

....

....

14 Did you have fun?

1 *Last Saturday*

A What did these people do last Saturday? Write sentences.

1. pay bills
2. vacuum
3. wash clothes
4. exercise
5. dust
6. work in the yard
7. shop for groceries
8. cook

1. *She paid bills.*
2. _____
3. _____
4. _____

5. _____
6. _____
7. _____
8. _____

B What did you do last Saturday? Write three sentences.

1. _____
2. _____
3. _____

2 **Ben is writing in his journal. Complete the sentences. Use the simple past form of the verbs in parentheses.**

Friday

What a great day! This afternoon, I
invited (invite) some friends over after
school. We _____ (stop) at the video
store, but we _____ (not get) a movie.
We _____ (play) basketball and
_____ (listen) to music. Mom
_____ (cook) some hamburgers for dinner.
After dinner, we _____ (watch) television.

Saturday

This morning, Kelly _____ (call).
She _____ (invite) me to her sister's
birthday party. I _____ (need) a present
for the party, so I _____ (walk) to
the mall. The party _____ (start)
at 7:00 and _____ (end) at 10:00.
Kelly and I _____ (dance) and
_____ (talk) all evening. She's really cool.

Sunday

I _____ (study) this morning.
In the afternoon, Mom, Dad, and I
_____ (shop) for groceries. Then I
_____ (help) Mom with dinner. After
dinner, I _____ (clean) my room. In
the evening, I _____ (call) Kelly, but we
_____ (not talk) very long. Tomorrow's a
school day, so I'm going to go to bed now.
Good night!

80 ● *Unit 14*

3 **Carol and Max did different things last weekend. Write sentences about them.**

1. study   *Carol studied. Max didn't study.*

2. clean the kitchen

3. play golf

4. cook

5. listen to music

6. walk in the park

7. watch television

4 *Complete the chart.*

Present	Past	Present	Past
buy	*bought*	go	_____
come	_____	have	_____
do	_____	read	_____
_____	ate	_____	rode
feel	_____	_____	saw
_____	got up	sit	_____

5 *Complete the conversation. Use the simple past forms of the verbs in parentheses.*

Kevin: So, Megan, _____*did*_____ you _____*have*_____ (have) a good summer?

Megan: Well, I _____ (have) an interesting summer. My sister
and her family _____ (visit) for two weeks.

Kevin: That's nice.

Megan: Yes and no. My sister _____ (not feel)
well, so she _____ (sit) on the sofa
and _____ (watch) television.
She hardly ever _____ (get up).

Kevin: Oh, well. _____ her husband and kids
_____ (have) a good time?

Megan: I think so. They _____ (play) volleyball
and _____ (ride) their bikes every day.

Kevin: _____ you _____ (go out) to
any restaurants?

Megan: No, I _____ (cook) breakfast, lunch,
and dinner every day. They _____ (eat)
a lot of food, but they _____ (not wash)
any dishes.

Kevin: That's too bad. _____ you
_____ (relax) at all last summer?

Megan: Yes. My sister and her family finally
_____ (go) home, and then I
_____ (relax). I just _____ (read)
some books and _____ (see) some movies.

6 *Unscramble the questions about last summer. Then answer with your own information.*

Last summer, . . . ?

1. go   interesting   anywhere   you   did

   A: _Did you go anywhere interesting?_

   B: _Yes, I did. I went to Hawaii./No, I didn't. I just stayed home._

2. any   take   did   you   pictures

   A: _____

   B: _____

3. buy   you   did   anything   interesting

   A: _____

   B: _____

4. did   eat   you   foods   any   new

   A: _____

   B: _____

5. games   did   you   any   play

   A: _____

   B: _____

6. you   did   sports   play   any

   A: _____

   B: _____

7. you   did   interesting   meet   any   people

   A: _____

   B: _____

8. did   any   books   you   read   good

   A: _____

   B: _____

9. any   see   you   did   movies   good

   A: _____

   B: _____

Summer activities

A Greg and Grant did different activities last summer. Write sentences about them.

1. *Greg got up early every day.*
2. _____
3. _____
4. _____
5. _____
6. _____
7. _____
8. _____

B Write sentences about your activities last summer.

1. _____
2. _____
3. _____
4. _____

15 Where were you born?

1 *Complete the conversation. Use the sentences in the box.*

☐ I was sixteen.	☐ No, it wasn't. I loved it.
☑ No, I wasn't. I was born in the Caribbean.	☐ No, I'm from the Dominican Republic.
☐ I came here to study English.	☐ I moved here in 2002.
☐ I was born in Puerto Plata.	☐ Yes, they were. We were all born there.

Melissa: Were you born here in the U.S., Luis?

Luis: *No, I wasn't. I was born in the Caribbean.*

Melissa: Oh, were you born in Cuba?

Luis: _____

Melissa: Really? What city were you born in?

Luis: _____

Melissa: Were your parents born in Puerto Plata, too?

Luis: _____

Melissa: And why did you come to the U.S.?

Luis: _____

Melissa: So when did you move here?

Luis: _____

Melissa: Really? How old were you then?

Luis: _____

Melissa: Was it scary?

Luis: _____

2 *Complete these conversations with* **was, wasn't, were,** *or* **weren't.**

1. Peter: I called you on Saturday, but you ___weren't___ home.

    David: No, I _____ . I _____ in the mountains
    all weekend.

    Peter: That's nice. How _____ the weather there?

    David: It _____ beautiful.

    Peter: _____ your parents there?

    David: No, they _____ . I _____ alone.
    It _____ great!

the mountains

Chicago

2. Sue: _____ you born in the U.S., Wendy?

    Wendy: Yes, I _____ . My brother and I
    _____ born here in New York.

    Sue: I _____ born here, too. What about
    your parents? _____ they born here?

    Wendy: Well, my father _____ . He _____
    born in China, but my mother _____
    born in the U.S. – in Chicago.

    Sue: Chicago? Really? My parents _____
    born in Chicago, too!

Nice

3. Nancy: _____ you in college last
    year, Chuck?

    Chuck: No, I _____ . I graduated from
    college two years ago.

    Nancy: So where _____ you last year?

    Chuck: I _____ in France.

    Nancy: Oh! _____ you in Paris?

    Chuck: No, I _____ . I _____
    in Nice. I had a job there.

    Nancy: What _____ the job?

    Chuck: I _____ a front desk agent at
    a hotel.

3 *Write four sentences about each person.*

1
Bruce Lee, actor
1940–1973
• born in the U.S.
• was in movie *Enter the Dragon,* 1973

2
Roberto Clemente, baseball player
1934–1972
• born in Puerto Rico
• became a member of the Baseball Hall of Fame, 1973

3
Marie Curie, scientist
1867–1934
• born in Poland
• won the Nobel Prize for Chemistry, 1911

4
Audrey Hepburn, actress
1929–1993
• born in Belgium
• was in movie *Breakfast at Tiffany's,* 1961

5
Georgia O'Keeffe, painter
1887–1986
• born in the U.S.
• painted *White Flower,* 1929

6
Ernest Hemingway, writer
1899–1961
• born in the U.S.
• wrote *The Old Man and the Sea,* 1952

1. *Bruce Lee was an actor. He was born in 1940 in the U.S.*
   He was in the movie Enter the Dragon *in 1973. He died in 1973.*

2. _____

3. _____

4. _____

5. _____

6. _____

4 **Are these classes easy, difficult, interesting, or boring? Complete the chart. Then add one more class to each column. (Some classes can go in more than one column.)**

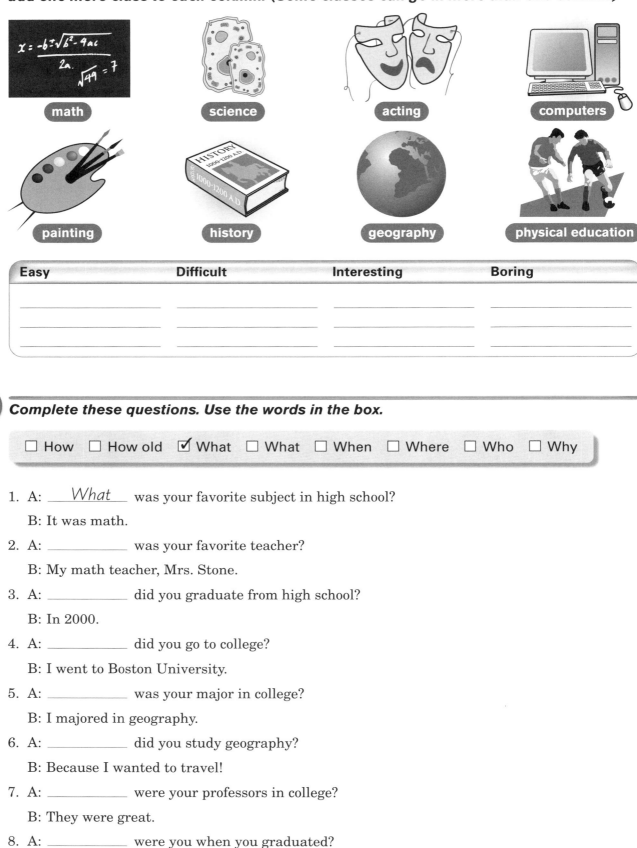

math   science   acting   computers

painting   history   geography   physical education

Easy	Difficult	Interesting	Boring

5 **Complete these questions. Use the words in the box.**

☐ How   ☐ How old   ☑ What   ☐ What   ☐ When   ☐ Where   ☐ Who   ☐ Why

1. A: ___*What*___ was your favorite subject in high school?

   B: It was math.

2. A: _____ was your favorite teacher?

   B: My math teacher, Mrs. Stone.

3. A: _____ did you graduate from high school?

   B: In 2000.

4. A: _____ did you go to college?

   B: I went to Boston University.

5. A: _____ was your major in college?

   B: I majored in geography.

6. A: _____ did you study geography?

   B: Because I wanted to travel!

7. A: _____ were your professors in college?

   B: They were great.

8. A: _____ were you when you graduated?

   B: I was 22 years old.

6 **Unscramble the questions about your elementary school days. Then answer with your own information.**

1. was   your   of school   how   first day

   A: _How was your first day of school?_____

   B: _____

2. your   was   teacher   who   favorite

   A: _____

   B: _____

3. favorite   was   your   what   class

   A: _____

   B: _____

4. your   who   best   were   friends

   A: _____

   B: _____

5. spend   did   your   where   you   free time

   A: _____

   B: _____

6. finish   did   when   you   elementary school

   A: _____

   B: _____

7 *Childhood memories*

A Complete the questions with *did*, *was*, or *were*.
Then answer the questions. Use short answers.

1. A: _____Were_____ you born here?

   B: _Yes, I was. / No, I wasn't._

2. A: _____ you grow up in a big city?

   B: _____

3. A: _____ both your parents work?

   B: _____

4. A: _____ your father serious?

   B: _____

5. A: _____ your mother talkative?

   B: _____

6. A: _____ you have a lot of friends?

   B: _____

7. A: _____ your best friend thin?

   B: _____

8. A: _____ you live in an apartment?

   B: _____

9. A: _____ your house or apartment

   large?

   B: _____

10. A: _____ you walk to school?

    B: _____

11. A: _____ you tall?

    B: _____

12. A: _____ you shy?

    B: _____

B Write sentences about your childhood.

1. _____

2. _____

3. _____

4. _____

5. _____

16 Can she call you later?

Make a phone conversation. Use the sentences and questions in the box.

Bill

Claire

☐ I'm sorry, she's not here right now.
☐ OK. Give me your number.
☐ No problem. Bye.
☐ Sure. What's the message?
☐ 555-0662. Got it.
☑ Hello?
☐ Oh, hi, Claire.

☐ Thanks, Bill.
☑ Hi, Bill. It's Claire.
☐ Oh. Can you give her a message?
☐ It's 555-0662.
☐ Please ask her to call me.
☐ Can I speak to Linda, please?
☐ Bye-bye.

Bill: *Hello?*

Claire: *Hi, Bill. It's Claire.*

Bill: _____

Claire: _____

Bill: _____

Claire: _____

Bill: _____

Claire: _____

Bill: _____

Claire: _____

Bill: _____

Claire: _____

Bill: _____

Claire: _____

2 Scott Gibson called his friends yesterday, but he didn't talk to them. Where were they? Complete the conversations with the words in the box.

☐ beach   ☐ class   ☐ hospital   ☑ library   ☐ mall   ☐ shower

Diego

1. Scott: Hello, Mrs. Gomez. It's Scott.
   Is Diego there, please?
   Mrs. Gomez: Oh, hello, Scott. No, I'm sorry,
   he isn't here. He's at the library.

Diane

2. Scott: Hi, Helen. _____
   _____
   Helen: Hi, Scott. No, I'm sorry, _____

Brian and Jane

3. Scott: Hi, Uncle Dave. _____
   _____
   Dave: How are you, Scott? No, I'm sorry,
   _____

Jordan

4. Scott: Hello. This is Scott Gibson.
   _____
   Man: No, I'm sorry, _____
   _____

Laurie

5. Scott: Hello, Mr. Lee. _____
   _____
   Mr. Lee: Hello, Scott. She's here, but _____
   _____

Ross and Dan

6. Scott: Hey, Joey. _____
   _____
   Joey: Hey, Scott. _____
   _____

3 *Subject and object pronouns*

A Complete the chart.

Subjects	Objects
I	*me*
_____	you
he	_____
she	_____
we	_____
_____	them

B Complete the sentences with the correct words in parentheses.

1. Please give it to _____ (he / him).

2. _____ (She / Her) isn't here right now.

3. Can _____ (I / me) help you?

4. Please leave _____ (we / us) a message.

5. _____ (They / Them) are in the library.

4 *Complete the answering machine messages with the correct pronouns.*

Answering machine

Hello, this is Jim. ___*I*___ can't come to the phone right now. Please leave ___*me*___ a message after the beep. *Beep!*

Bob's message

Hi, Jim. This is Bob. My sister Olivia is visiting _____ . Do you remember _____ ? Well, _____ 're going to have lunch at Carol's Café tomorrow. Can you meet _____ there? Please call _____ today.

Jim's message

Hi, Bob. I'm sorry I missed your call. Well, _____ can't meet _____ and Olivia for lunch tomorrow, but maybe you can meet _____ after work. My friends and I are going to go out to a great pizza restaurant. Would you like to join _____ ? Give _____ a call!

5 **Complete the phone conversation. Use the words in the box.**

☐ at ☐ call ☐ does ☐ her ☐ please
☐ but ☑ can ☐ have ☐ in ☐ this

Sam: Hello?

Ray: Hello. ___Can___ I speak to

Carol, _____ ?

Sam: I'm sorry, _____ she can't come

to the phone right now.

She's _____ the yard. Can I

give _____ a message?

Ray: Yes. _____ is Ray Santos.

Please ask her to _____ me.

I'm _____ work.

Sam: Does she _____ the number?

Ray: Yes, she _____ .

6 **Complete the excuses. Use your own ideas.**

1. A: Can you watch my dog Bitsy on Sunday?
   B: I'm sorry, but I can't. I have to _visit my parents._

2. A: Do you want to go to the library this weekend?
   B: I'd like to, but I need to _____

3. A: Can you cook dinner for me this evening?
   B: I'm sorry, but I have to _____

4. A: Can you help me with my homework tonight?
   B: I'm sorry, but I can't. I have to _____

5. A: Would you like to go to the laundromat on Saturday?
   B: I'd like to, but I need to _____

6. A: Can you clean my apartment this weekend?
   B: I'm sorry, but I have to _____

7 Imagine your friends are inviting you to do these things. Accept or refuse their invitations. Use the phrases in the chart.

Accepting	Refusing and making excuses
I'd love to.	I'm sorry, but I can't. I have to / need to / want to . . .
I'd like to.	Gee. I'd like to, but I have to / need to / want to . . .

1. A: Do you want to go to the art gallery this afternoon?

   B: _____

2. A: Do you want to have dinner with me tomorrow night?

   B: _____

3. A: Do you want to watch television at my house next Wednesday?

   B: _____

4. A: Do you want to go dancing with me on Saturday night?

   B: _____

5. A: Do you want to go hiking with me this weekend?

   B: _____

8 Write each sentence a different way. Use the sentences in the box.

☑ Hi, this is Amy.   ☐ I'm busy.   ☐ Do you want to see a movie?
☐ Is Barbara there?   ☐ I'd like to go to the movies.   ☐ Can I take a message?

1. Hi, it's Amy.
   Hi, this is Amy. _____

2. Can I speak with Barbara?

   _____

3. Would you like to go to the movies?

   _____

4. I want to go to the movies.

   _____

5. I have other plans.

   _____

6. Do you want to leave a message?

   _____

9 *Answer the questions. Write sentences with* like to, want to, *and* need to.

Example: What are two things you want to do tomorrow?

I want to exercise for two hours tomorrow morning.

I want to relax in the afternoon.

1. What are two things you like to do often?

_____

_____

2. Where are two places you want to visit?

_____

_____

3. Who are two famous people you want to meet?

_____

_____

4. What are two things you need to do this week?

_____

_____

5. Where are two places you like to go on weekends?

_____

_____

6. What are two things you need to do in class?

_____

_____

7. What are two things you like to do in class?

_____

_____

8. What are two things you want to do in your next class?

_____

_____